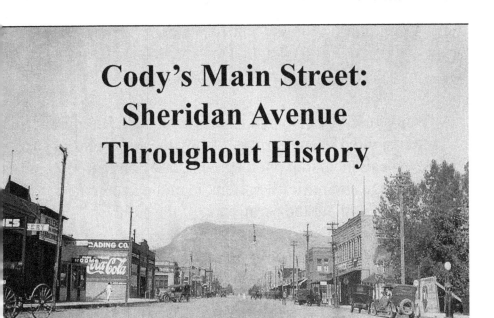

Cody's Main Street: Sheridan Avenue Throughout History

By
Todd S. Valley

Library of Congress Control Number: 2018910927
ISBN: 978-1717315267
Copyright 2018 Todd S. Valley

Permission may be granted by contacting:
Todd S. Valley
213 F. Street
Cody, WY 82414

Printed by Createspace, An Amazon Company

The majority of the photos in this manuscript are protected by copyright and are available from:
Park County Archives
1501 Stampede Avenue
Unit 9001
Cody, WY 82414
(307) 527-8530

Acknowledgements

I would like to thank the following individuals and organizations for their assistance in compiling the histories and images included in this book.

Park County Historical Archives
McCracken Research Center at Buffalo Bill Center of the West
American Heritage Center-University of Wyoming
Wyoming State Archives
Bob Wilson
Jon Wilson
Gale Hill
Lynn Johnson Houze
Janet Frost Bucknell for photos and editing this manuscript

Books Used For Research

Houze, Lynn Johnson. 2011 *Then and Now Cody*. Charleston SC: Arcadia Publishing
Hicks, Lucille N. 1980. *The Park County Story*. Dallas, TX: Taylor Publishing Co.

Introduction

This book will document the changes of businesses along Codys Main Street, Sheridan Avenue. This book covers mainly the years beginning in the 1930's and progressing until 2018. There are a few businesses that I was able to obtain earlier pictures of and so those businesses will have more of their individual history. Early pictures of Cody are very rare and often times are either hard to find or don't exist anymore.

If you have any historic or recent pictures of Cody, whether downtown or general Cody pictures, the Park County Archives would enjoy the opportunity to borrow them to scan or would welcome the donation of these pictures. Pictures may be taken to:

Park County Archives
1501 Stampede Avenue
Unit 9001
Cody, Wy 82414
(307) 527-8530

About The Author

Todd S. Valley was born in Morro Bay, California in 1961. In 1971, He moved to Coalinga, California where he resided until 1986. While living in California, he developed a love for history and historic structures and sites.

After graduating from West Hills Community College in 1986 with an Associate of Arts Degree, he moved to Topeka, Kansas. While living in Topeka, Kansas he would increase his love for history and historic buildings.

In 1990, he published his first manuscript "The Oregon Trail in Topeka: Focusing on Anthony and Mary Jane Ward".

In 2006, he moved to Cody, Wyoming, where he currently resides.

Brief history of the founding of Cody

The town of Cody was originally founded in 1896 near what was DeMaris Hot Springs, about two miles west of the current location of the city of Cody. The city was founded by seven individuals: George T. Beck, Nate Salsbury, Harry Gerrans, Bronson Rumsey, Horace Alger, George Bleistein and Buffalo Bill Cody. Due to problems with land ownership and Charles DeMaris's reluctance to sell any land, the town was moved to its current location in 1896.

One event that helped spur the growth of the town of Cody was the interest of the Chicago, Burlington and Quincy Railroad in building a spur line from Toluca, Montana to Cody. The founders of Cody, in agreement with the C, B, and Q Railroad sold a majority of the then-existing town lots to the railroad. The railroad was completed and opened on November 19, 1901.

Cody was originally in Big Horn County until 1909, when Cody had a large enough population for recognition as the county seat and the area to become Park County.

Since the time of the railroad reaching Cody, the town has been constantly growing and changing to become the city that it is today.

Built 1909

1940

Cody Cottages — Opposite Buffalo Bill Museum
U. S. Highway 14 and 20
Cody, Wyoming

1967

LINDYS
EAT-O-RAMA

1980's

875 Sheridan Avenue

This site was the home of Frank Houx, Cody's first Mayor. His house was built on this location in 1909. In 1996 the Houx house was moved to 1413 Rumsey Avenue. From 1940-1948 this location served as Cody Cottages. In 1967-1969 this location was Lindy's Eat-O-Rama. In 1971 this address became Keller's Kitchen. From 1972-1993 this building was known as Eugene's Pizza. Big Horn Basin Regional Cancer Center now occupies this area.

7

Circa 1924

1932

Circa 1935

1936

937 Sheridan Avenue

This building was originally built in 1908 by Solon Wiley in Wiley, Wyoming and was called "Cliffs Ranch", where it was used as a residence and the Wiley State Bank. The town of Wiley, Wyoming was located about 10 miles southeast from Cody near the Oregon Basin Oilfields.

The ranch house was bought by Bob Trimble around 1931 and had to be transported to Cody in 2 pieces. This move would take the moving contractor over a year as it was winter time and also due to the fact that there were no paved roads in Wiley at the time.

Circa 1938

1946

2011

2018

937 Sheridan Avenue (continued)

In 1931, after its move to Cody, this structure was turned into an inn, known as the Trumbull Inn, owned by Bob Trumbull.

In 1963, this building became the Green Gables Inn, which offered rooms and apartments for rent for several years. Later the exterior porch was enclosed and turned into a dining room.

The house was renamed The Green Gables Inn and Pancake House from 1966-1989. It became Tag's on 10th between 1990-1992. This building was sold and became Maxwell's restaurant between 1992-2012. It is Currently home to China Town Buffet.

1001-1007 Sheridan Avenue

From the time this structure was built, it served as Red Horse Service Station under many owners. In 1982-1983, this building evolved into a restaurant site, first known as the Burger Inn. During 1984-2014, this storefront was home to Taco John's Owned by Robin and Connie Dallman. Since 2015, this building has been home to Rocky Mountain Mojoes.

1015 Sheridan Avenue

Between the years of 1936-1956, this address was one of Cody's early auto court motels, The Green Gables Auto Court.

From 1956-2002, this location became a motel known as Mountaineer Court. In 2004-2010, this location became Econolodge Moose Creek Inn. Since 2011, this address has been home to Moose Creek Inn and Suites.   11

1906

1917

1920

1057 Sheridan Avenue

Cody's first Library was built on this location in 1906 at a cost of $1350. The building was 16x16. It opened on November 11, 1906. The library was only open on Tuesday afternoons and all day and evening on Saturday.

The second library on this property was built and opened on May 9, 1916 and was one of the Carnegie libraries built across the country.

1965

2018

2018

1057 Sheridan Avenue (continued)

In 1964 the second library was torn down and replaced with a newer building. The new library would remain in this location until 2008, when the library moved to the lower level of the former Marathon Oil Company building.

The new Cody Public Library is located at 1500 Heart Mountain Street and is also home to the Park County Archives.

Bill DeMaris

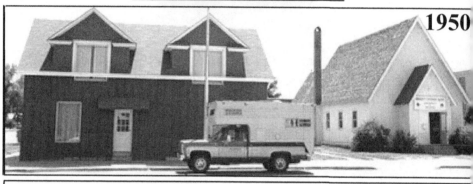

1950

2018

1092 Sheridan Avenue

This location has been home to the DeMaris house since 1907. Charles DeMaris built the house at this location. It originally contained 10 rooms. DeMaris owned the hot springs about 3 miles west of town. the family moved to town when Bill DeMaris was about 6 years old.

The house has been a real estate office and was used as offices for the Cody fire department. Since May of 2018 it has become the Cody Heritage Museum which highlights the history of Cody.

Circa 1942

1979

1984

2018

1101 Sheridan Avenue

This location was home to several Sinclair Gas Stations between 1940-1972.

From 1977-1982, this address was home to Daylight Donuts, which also served pizza, ice cream, sandwiches and coffee.

In the years of 1983-1992 this location became Murray's Apothecary, a locally owned and operated drug store. This drug store was run by Roger and Love Murray.

Since 1993 this address has been home to Maurice's, a womens clothing store.   15

Circa 1924

1924

Ned Frost

1145 Sheridan Avenue

Around 1920-1921, Ned Frost built his Studebaker Garage and dealership. He also built Frost Curio for his wife, Mary at this location.

He would continue to run this business until 1948-1949. In 1949, this building became Cody Garage.

Cody Garage remained at this address until 1951. During the years of 1951-1953, this address became an office complex.

1949

1978

1978

2018

1145 Sheridan Avenue (continued)

In 1978, this building became the storefront for Western Real Estate and the Copper Rivet, a clothing store. Between 1992-1993 this was home to Simply Unique. From 2004-2015 this address was home to Mountain Made Treasures. This address is currently the storefronts for Western Real Estate and Monie's. There are several businesses located in the interior hallway.

Mary Frost

NED FROST GUIDE AND
CURIO DEALER

STOP AT THE
RICHARD RANCH
HALFWAY TO THE PARK

1930's

Circa 1932

1145 Sheridan Avenue

Mary Frost started Frost Curio around 1917-1918. The business was originally located in the Irma Hotel in the area that is now the Silver Saddle Lounge.

Mary also had a second location inside the Burlington Inn at the Cody train depot. Mary sold traditional Native American rugs, pottery and bead work which she purchased from the Native Americans in the area, as well as import goods and souvenirs.

Later in the 1920's, her husband built a Studebaker dealership across the street and she moved her curio shop into a portion of that building.   18

FROST CURIO SHOP
"THAT WHICH IS REAL"

IN THE STUDEBAKER BLDG.

THE BIGGEST STOCK OF ITS
KIND IN WYOMING

We are always glad to have visitors

INDIAN THINGS--OLD AND NEW
Indian Novelties---50c to $500
YELLOWSTONE SOUVENIRS
CODY SOUVENIRS

Things that are different from all
over the world

MEN	WOMEN	CHILDREN
BELTS	BLANKETS	CHAPS
HATS	NAVAJO RUGS	HATS
HAT BANDS	SERAPPYS	VESTS
BILL FOLDS	CHIMAYO	CUFFS
HANDKERCIF'S	JEWELRY	GUNS
SLIPPERS	PURSES	KNIVES
MOCCASINS	PILLOWS	MARBLES
KNIVES	LEATHER GOODS	BEAR
PIPES	LAMPS	MONKEYS
VESTS	BOOKENDS	INDIAN DOLLS
SMOK. SETS	CANDLE STICKS	TIE RACKS
CIGARET BOXES	BASKETS	TIE HOLDERS

Come in and see the many things not listed.

1924

2018

1145 Sheridan Avenue (continued)

Mary ran the Frost Curio Shop in this location until 1952, when she sold the business to her son Richard "Dick" Frost. Dick would move this business to the corner of 12th and Sheridan.

Mary initially ran this business in the summer while the men were working at the Frost Ranch on the Fork or were guiding hunting trips. After moving into town from the ranch, she would run this business year round.   19

BRUNDAGE HARDWARE COMPANY.
A. J. MARTIN, President   R. J. McGINNIS, Secretary-Treasurer.

1932

1932

Circa 1935

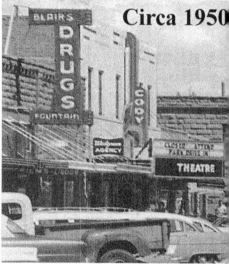

Circa 1950

1161 Sheridan Avenue

This structure was built in 1932 and was home to Wilson Drug Store until 1936.

In 1936, this building would become Brundage Hardware until 1938.

From 1938-1964, this storefront was the location of Blair's Drug Store. The drug store was owned and operated by Quin Blair.

1968

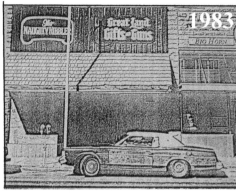

1983

2018

1161 Sheridan Avenue (continued)

From 1965-1971 this building was home to the Apothecary Shop. In 1976 Bucking Horse Gallery occupied this building.

In 1983-1984 this address was home to The Naughty Nibbler and Great Land Gifts and Guns. This building became the store front of the Real Thing from 1984-1985. Since 2002 this store front has been home to Simpson Gallagher Gallery.

Circa 1925

Circa 1925

Circa 1925

1169 Sheridan Avenue

The Park Garage was built on this location sometime in the early 1920's. The Park Garage would close somewhere around 1936.

The new owner of the property was Earl Corder. He would turn this property into the Cody Theatre, by tearing off the roof, redoing the inside of the building and adding a second floor with a curved roof. The movie theatre opened on July 8, 1937.

During the time that this address has been the Cody Theatre, at least four world or regional premieres have been held here.

Circa 1925

2006

2009

2009

1167-1169 Sheridan Avenue

When Corder built the theatre, he did not want a snack bar in the building. The patrons would buy their tickets and go next door to the fountain and get their snacks. Earl would let you in with candy, popcorn, and soft drinks.

The fountain and the small buildings on each end would be rented out and over the years would be home to many businesses. Some of these businesses would include a psychic card reader, several clothing stores and even insurance and real estate agencies.

23

1167-1169 Sheridan Avenue (continued)

John Schultz leased the theatre from Corder in 1963. He purchased it in 1968 and ran it until 1992.

In 1992 Schultz sold the building to Bob and Sandy Newsome, who still own the building. The last movie shown in the theatre was "The Great Debaters" in 2007.

From 2007-2015 Dan Miller rented the building for Dan Miller's Cowboy Music Review. In 2016 Newsome's son, Wiley, took over operation of the theatre and began showing movies in the building again. Wiley ran movies in the building during 2016-2017. The building is now rented for dance shows and is used for many community events.   24

Circa 1904

Circa 1906

Circa 1960

1977

1191 Sheridan Avenue

This structure was one of the first business buildings built in Cody. The Walls building was constructed around 1904. This building was the office of W.L. Walls. Walls was one of the early lawyers in Cody.

This address has served as one of the first banks built in Cody. The bank was First National Bank at the time.

On November 1, 1904, in the afternoon, this bank was robbed by two men who entered the front door to the bank. The robbers tried to hold up Ira O. Midaugh, the cashier. Midaugh ran out a side door onto 12th street and was murdered in the street by one of the robbers.

1191 Sheridan Avenue (continued)

By 1960, this address was home to First State Bank, one of several banks that would call this address home.

From 1992-1994 this building was home to Town Bakery and Sub Shoppe. Between 1995-2004 this address was the first location of Peter's Cafe and Bakery. It would then become the storefront for two art galleries until 2010.

Since 2010 this building has been home to Sean Denamur Jewelers and Design.

Circa 1930's

Circa 1953

1961

1201 Sheridan Avenue

In the early 1920's, this corner was the location of the New York Store, one of Cody's early original grocery and variety stores.

From 1932-1951 this building was the Home Supply Store which sold everything from groceries to appliances.

During the years of 1952-1961 this address became the location for Frost Curio. Richard "Dick" Frost had purchased this business from his mother Mary Frost.　　　　27

Dick Frost

Circa 1954

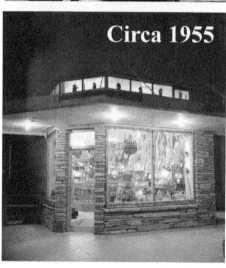
Circa 1955

Circa 1955

1201 Sheridan Avenue

After purchasing the Frost Curio business from his mother Mary Frost in 1952, Richard "Dick" Frost opened the shop at 1201 Sheridan Avenue. He would continue to run this business until the mid 1960's.

At one point he also had a second location known as the Buffalo Bill Shop which was located at 1607 8th street, (now Yellowstone Avenue north of where Dairy Queen is today.

Circa 1953

1950's

1607 8th Street

1201 Sheridan Avenue (continued)

Frost Curio was always a popular curio shop in cody, both when owned by Mary Frost and later by Dick Frost.

Frost Curio was well known for selling a wide variety of items and catering to the tourist trade to Yellowstone National Park.

Dick was involved in many of the fraternal organizations in Cody, including the Cody Club.

Dick was the second Curator of the Buffalo Bill Museum and was responsible for hiring Dr. Harold McCracken to create the Whitney Gallery of Art at the Museum.   29

Circa 1965

1980

1993

2018

1201 Sheridan Avenue (continued)

From 1962-1967 this address was First Curio and First Frontier Store. From 1969-1976 the building was the Royal Sporting Goods Store.

The Great American Ice Cream Company and Restaurant occupied this location between 1978-1989.

From 1990-2003 this storefront was home to Mountain West Trading Company.

Since 2006 this building has been the business location for Open Range Images, a local photography gallery and store. 30

1905

1905

BENNETT'S CODY DRUG & JEWELRY COMPANY.
W. S. BENNETT, M. D., Prop.
Kodak Supplies   Fishing Tackle   Curios

1921

1985

1202 Sheridan Avenue

This building was built around 1904. In 1905, Dr. William Sabin Bennett opened a medical practice on the second floor and Cody Drug and Jewelry on the main floor. Bennett's slogan was "Bennett Handles The Goods." His logo was a small red cross.

He was elected to the school board in 1912 and as mayor of Cody in 1913. He was one of the first men to own a car in Cody. In 1919 he was elected as Public Health Officer for Park County. In 1912 he sold his business to Dr. Trueblood. Dr. Bennett was known for driving fast and also for his affairs with Cassie Waters.   31

1985

1986

2012

2018

1202 Sheridan Avenue (continued)

It is believed that at one time there may have been a brothel upstairs and, during prohibition, a speakeasy in the basement.

The building then became home to Cody Corral from 1951-1956. From 1964-1978 this building was known as Cody Corral Western Wear. During 1979-1994 the name was changed to Corral West. This address then became home to Seidel's Saddlery, owned and operated by Keith Seidel. In 2016 the storefront became Annie's Old Fashioned Soda Saloon, owned by Jeanette Prosceno. Keith still maintains Seidel's saddlery in the upstairs of the building.   32

1209 Sheridan Avenue

When this building was first built, it was the office of one of Cody's early doctors, Dr. Ainsworth.

In 1932, this address became home to Edward's Bakery. In 1933 this building was home to the Square Deal Grocery Store. It was also once part of the New York Store.

Between the years of 1938-1947 it was a local pool hall known as the OK Pool Hall.

1954

1955

1948

1970

1209 Sheridan Avenue (continued)

In 1948 this building became the store front for the Snack and Cue, a restaurant and local pool hall. Between 1952-1956 this building was home to Craig's Cafe. Craig's would remain at this location until it moved to the 1400 block of Sheridan. From 1970-1971 this address was an appliance and television store known as Sedam's Appliance and TV.

1209 Sheridan Avenue (continued)

From 1971-1992 this building was the location of the local Sears Catalog Merchandise store.

Between 1993 and 2001, this address was home to Scary Mary's, a women's clothing and accessories store.

In 2016, this store front became U Blaze, an electronic cigarette and electronic vapor store.

Circa 1905

1940's

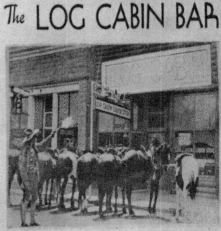
The LOG CABIN BAR

CODY --- BUFFALO BILL'S HOME

1212 Sheridan Avenue

This building was originally built around 1903-1904 by R.A. Roth as the Buffalo Hump Saloon. From 1936-1951 this location was home to a popular drinking establishment, The Log Cabin Bar.

In 1951 this store front became the location on Loyd's Spudnuts, this location remained a donut shop until 1956.

Between that time and 1978 there have been several establishments at this address. 36

1950

THERE'S A SPUDNUT SHOP IN YOUR TOWN
TAKE A DOZEN HOME TODAY!

Meet Mr. Spudnut!

AMERICA'S FINEST FOOD CONFECTION

1985

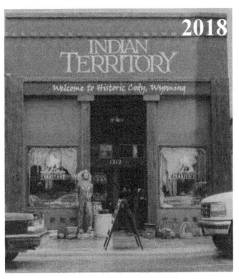

2018

INDIAN TERRITORY

Welcome to Historic Cody, Wyoming

1212 Sheridan Avenue (continued)

From 1978-1993 this location was Bear Butt Clothing Store owned and operated by Barb and Freddie Martin.

In 2002 it became Indian Territory, a Native American store and art gallery where it remains today.

Circa 1938

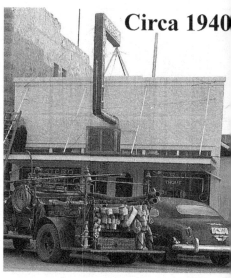

Circa 1940

1976

1213 Sheridan Avenue

From 1937-1952 this store front was home to Western Grill. This restaurant was one of three next door to each other. The other two being Craig's Cafe on the west and Mayflower Cafe on the east.

Between 1953 and 1960 this building was home to two different clothing stores.

In 1960 this location became the storefront for Michel's Jewelry, which would remain at this address until 1976.   38

Circa 1975

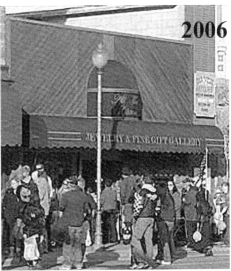

2006

2017

1213 Sheridan Avenue

From 1961-1976 Hoffman Typewriter Company also occupied this building at the same time as Michel's Jewelry.

During 1977-1979 this location was Thunderhorse Gallery. From 1980-2006 this address was home to Cody Jewelers. In 2007-2014 this business was known as All That Glitters.

Between 2015-2016 this building became Golden Buffalo.

Since 2016, this address has once again become home to Cody Jewelers.　　　39

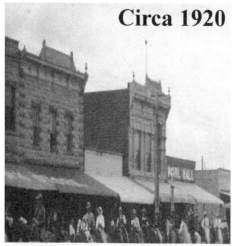
Circa 1920

Circa 1922

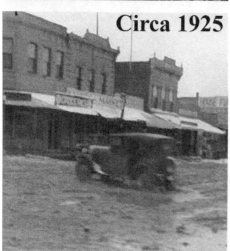
Circa 1925

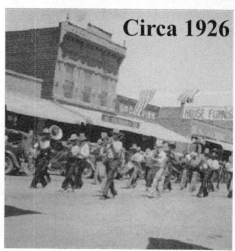
Circa 1926

1219 Sheridan Avenue

Fred Barnett constructed this business in 1904 and the second floor was used as a community center for the city.

This building was originally called Barnett Hall, but was later renamed Kath Hall. It was named for the gentleman whostaged sporting events on the second floor.

On the main floor was John Thompson's Cash Store. The store slogan was "Dry Goods and Ladies' and Gents' Furnishings."

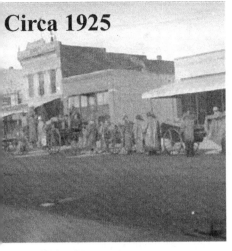

Circa 1925

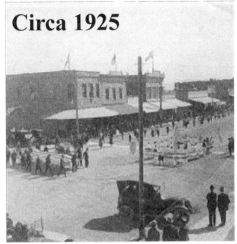

Circa 1925

1942

1965

1219 Sheridan Avenue (continued)

In 1911 the store became Humphries Dry Goods Store with Agnes Volkmer running the millinery department. In 1913, Volkmer took over the building and ran her millinery shop in it until 1932.

Louis Kousoulos Sr opened the first Mayflower Cafe in 1935 and ran it until 1959. Louis sold the business to his son Louis, Jr. After 1964, Louis and his wife remodeled the upstairs and opened The Golden Eagle Cafe, which was a fine dining establishment. They still owned and operated the Mayflower Cafe on the main floor.

1968

1989

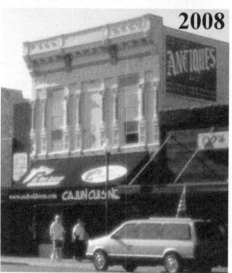

2008

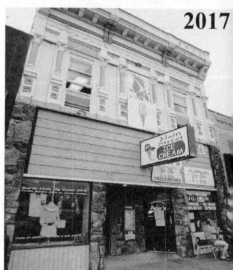

2017

1219 Sheridan Avenue (continued)

In 1977, the Golden Eagle closed and became Klaar's Mens Store. The Mayflower Cafe remained in business until 1983.

For a short time in 2008-2009 this address was home to Tommy Jack's Cajun Cuisine Restaurant.

Since 2009, Peter's Cafe and Main Street Ice Cream have remained in business at this location.

1950's

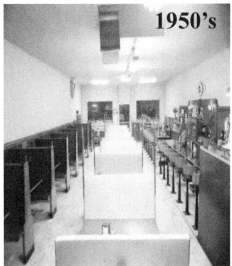
1950's

2005

2018

1220 Sheridan Avenue

This building was the original home of the Log Cabin Cafe in 1936. Between 1941-1965 this address was home to the Range Cafe.

From 1977-1985 this location was home to Park County Title. In 1992-2006 this storefront was Making Tracks, a clothing and T shirt shop.

Since 2011 this structure has been home to Rockstar Cowgirl.

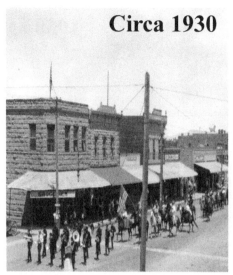
Circa 1930

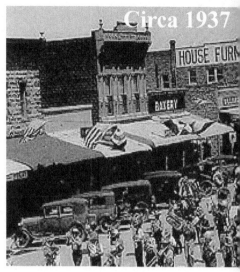
Circa 1937

1945

1955

1225 Sheridan Avenue

Originally this location was a grocery store in the 1930's.

Between 1936-1940 this location was home to Eddie's Bakery and then Cody Bakery.

From 1952-1985 this storefront was home to Cody Sporting Good, run by Bill Alsup. The store never had a sign out front saying Cody Sporting Goods. The sign had logos for Botany 500, Head, White Stag, Jantzen and McGregor .

1980

1981

CODY SPORTING GOODS

YOUR SPORTING GOODS
HEADQUARTERS

Bill Alcup

EVERYTHING FOR THE SPORTSMAN

CODY, WYOMING

2006

2018

1225 Sheridan Avenue (continued)

From 1996-2009 this address was home to JR's Fashions For Men, owned and operated by Jerry Posey.

Between 2014-2015 this location was Moose On The Loose.

Since 2015 this building has been the storefront for Yellowstone Out West, one of Cody's local T shirt shops.

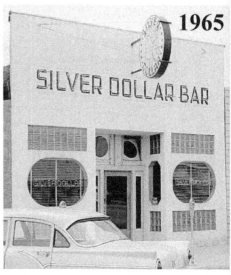

1226 Sheridan Avenue

From 1932-1933, this building was The Mint Cafe and Bar.

This building then became home to one of Cody's popular bars, The Silver Dollar Bar. The bar was in this location from 1962-1967 when the business moved to its current location.

In 2001, this storefront became B-Dazzled which remained in business until 2017.

Since 2018, this location has been home to Cody Custom Designs.

1946

1950's

2018

1227 Sheridan Avenue

This building is one of a few buildings on Sheridan Avenue that has not had many businesses in it.

This structure started out as Grupp's Cafe from 1936-1941.

In 1944 this address became Jimmie's Place Package Liquor Store. Then from 1945-1984 this address became another popular drinking establishment in Cody, The Wonder Bar.

Since 1985 this location has been home to the Proud Cut Saloon and Steak House.   47

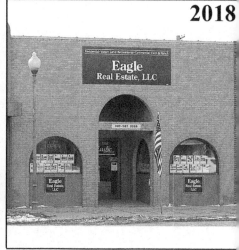

1234 Sheridan Avenue

This structure, when it was originally built, was a 2-story structure. Between 1941-1945 this address was the Coney Island Cafe, one of Cody's early cafes.

From 1960 to 1971 it was home to three different bakeries and also housed Browne's Barbershop which was owned and operated by "Brownie" Browne.

During the years of 1990-1991, this address was a sporting goods store known as Alpine Style Outdoor Store.

Since 2003, this address has been home to Eagle Real Estate.

Circa 1930's

1967

1976

1980

1236 Sheridan Avenue

This structure was originally built as Shuler's Market, one of Cody's early grocery stores from 1936-1937. From 1937-1941 this address was Wirt's Food Market. In 1947-1953 the structure became Wigwam Bakery before becoming Eddie's Bakery in 1956.

During the years of 1966-1970 this was home to Cody's T Bar C store. In 1976-1978 this address was home to The Country Store and then Champ's Chap Company.

 **1990**

 **1998**

 **2009**

 **2018**

1236 Sheridan Avenue (continued)

In 1990 this storefront became Morning Star Indian Gallery. Then in 1998 this became Morning Star Hobbies, Crafts and Books.

Later, in 2006, this address became the location of Buffalo Billie's Toy Store and Absaroka Cruise and Travel.

Between 2015-2017 this building was Grizzly Jim's.

Since 2017 this address has been home to Cody Trading Company with the motto "We Sell Things."

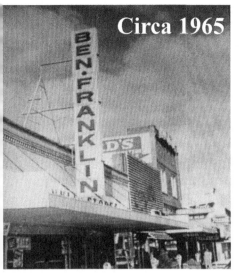

1237 Sheridan Avenue

From 1932-1944 this address was home to the Pastime Billiard Parlor. Prior to 1932 this location had been a bowling alley, but that building burned down and was replaced with the current structure.

In 1947 this building became the Ben Franklin Store and which remained until 1971. During 1972-1978 this address was the Yellowstone V Store. From 1979-1983 this building was the Yellowstone Store. Since 1984, it has been known as the Yellowstone Gift Shop.

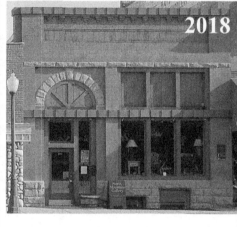

1241 Sheridan Avenue

This building was originally built in 1907 as the Stock Growers Bank. At that time the Wyoming National Guard had their armory in the basement and also did training there.

In around 1909, William Simpson opened Simpson Donley Law Firm at this location.

From 1985-2003 this structure was home to Holm, Blough and Company a local consulting engineering and land surveying firm. Since 2017 this address has been home to North Mountain Trails Gallery.   52

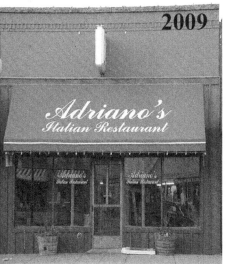
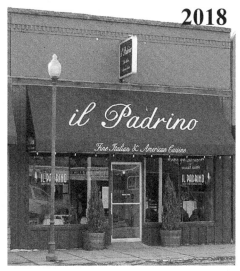

1244 Sheridan Avenue

In 1945 this address was home to Ben Franklin Variety Store. From 1947-1949 this structure was the Pastime Billiard Parlor. It would remain as a billiard parlor until 1964 under different names.

Between 1965-1983 this storefront was the Sportsman's Cafe. In 1984 it became Hong Kong Cafe. Between 2004-2017 this building was known as Adriano's Italian Restaurant. In 2017, after remodeling this storefront became home to Il Padrino, owned and operated by Stephen P. O'Donnell.   53

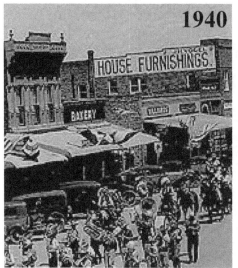
1940

1947

1962

1965

1251 Sheridan Avenue

Built around 1924, this structure was the J.H. Vogel Furniture Company until 1945. Vogel also ran a funeral parlor upstairs in the building. The owls on the front symbolized an undertaker or funeral parlor.

Between 1945-1956 this building was Marshall-Wells Store. This store sold everything from plumbing supplies to furniture, sporting goods and clothing.

In 1960, this address became home to Olson's Hardware which remained in business until 1963. During the years of 1962-1969 this building housed KODI Radio Station.   54

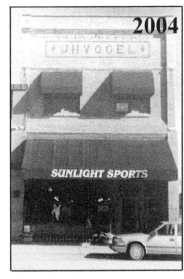

1251 Sheridan Avenue (continued)

From 1964-1989 this storefront was known as Howard's, then Howard's Western Wear.

In 1990-2006 this building served as the location for Sunlight Sports. In 2007 this address became Reindeer Ranch Gift Store which remained in business until 2013.

Since 2014 this building has been home to The Cowboy Palace, a local western wear and gift shop.

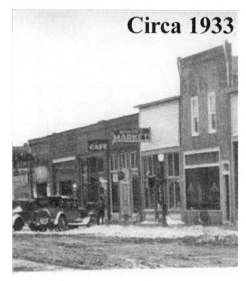

Circa 1933

Circa 1940

Circa 1940

1262 Sheridan Avenue

The Dave Jones building was built around 1924. It housed the Dave Jones Clothing Store from 1932-1941. In 1944, this business became Dave Jones Cleaners.

Dave Jones' business slogan was "Buy It Of Dave Jones". This slogan was very popular and could be found around the country, even painted on rocks, on signs in fields and sides of buildings. Soldiers even painted the slogan on rocks in England.

Circa 1948

1944

2018

1262 Sheridan Avenue (continued)

Between the years of 1945-1983, this structure was Western Clothiers. They had a slogan that they had "All Kinds Of Hand Tooled Leather Goods".

From 1987-2002 this address was Cody Quilt Company. In 2003 this building became Whispering Woods until 2008.

In 2010-2011 this was Grizzly Country Outdoors before becoming Shirt Off My Back in 2012.

Since 2013, this address has been home to Native Images.

1924

1924

"Frenchy" Sanders

Circa 1950's

1273 Sheridan Avenue

Around 1924, this building was home to the Palace Meat Market, with the Diamond Bar occupying the east end of the building.

Prior to 1924 this address was home to Cash's Store.

From 1935-1953 this building became primarily the drinking establishment known as the Diamond Bar.

The Diamond Bar was owned and operated by Kristen "Frenchy" Sanders.

1950's

1945

2018

1273 Sheridan Avenue (continued)

Between 1995-2006 this storefront was home to many businesses, including several real estate agencies, an auction company and a water garden business.

In 2007 the building was remodeled and the new building now encompasses what was three separate buildings before.

Since 2007 this address has been home to Love's Gifts And Other Things, which was formerly owned by Roger and Love Murray.

Circa 1975

Bustles 'n Bows

MUSTARD'S LAST STAND HOTDOGS

2006

WYOMING'S FINEST HOTDOG SHOP

2006

2018

1276 Sheridan Avenue

In 1940-1950 this address was home to Kerper and Kerper Law Firm.

From 1965-1977 this structure served as Bustles "n Bows Women's Clothing Shop. During the years of 1978-1980 the building became The House Special, before becoming The Elf Shelf from 1981-1985. In 1997-2000 this address was the storefront of Wyoming Buffalo Company. During 2001-2008 this building was Mustard's Last Stand, owned by Linda Boggiano. Since 2011 it has been Peaks to Prairie Realty. 60

1906

1953

1953

2018

1284-1286 Sheridan Avenue

Prior to 1907, this corner was known as Woodman's Hall. In 1907 there was a fire that destroyed all the wood-framed building on the block. In 1912, this corner became First National Bank. The bank was renamed First State Bank in 1932. The Golden Rule opened next door. From 1960-1989 this storefront was home to Cody Drug, before becoming Custom Cowboy shop and the Village Shoppe in 1990.

 1902

 Circa 1930

 Circa 1954

 2018

1291 Sheridan Avenue

Beginning on Jan 1, 1901-1956 This address was the location of Shoshone National Bank. Milward Simpson had his office in this building between 1936-1937.

During the years of 1960-1992 this bank became Shoshone First National Bank of Cody. From 1970-1977, Big Horn Computer Center also occupied space in the building.

From 1996-2005 this location was home to the Cody Rodeo Company. Between 2002-2005 this address was also home to Cody Hat Company.

Since 2006 this building has been the storefront for H&B Trading Post, owned by Herb and Barbara Hoy.

1907 1938

1938

Circa 1950

1301-1305 Sheridan Avenue

This structure was originally built in 1907 as the Newton Company General Store. The Pitchfork Club and Cafe occupied the second floor between 1936-1938. From 1937-1940 the main floor served as the Safeway Grocery Store.

This address then became Dungan's Upholstery and Furniture Store between 1940 and 1948.

From 1948-1964 this structure was home to the VR Trading Post. The VR stood for Vaughn Ragsdale. 63

1966

1980

2009

2018

1301-1305 Sheridan Avenue (continued)

During the years of 1965-1982 this structure was home to C.R. Anthony and then Anthony's, a clothing store. Between 1988-1994, 1305 was the location ofComputerland, while 1301 was Century 21 between the years of 1995-2003. From 2004-2009 this was ERA Beartooth Realty. From 2007-2015, 1305 was the Alltel Cell Phone Store. In 2016 this building became White Buffalo Clothing Store. Since 2018, 1301 has been home to the Christian Science Reading Room.

Circa 1910

After The Fire 1913

1920

1948

1302-1310 Sheridan Avenue

Cody Trading Company was founded in 1898 by Jake Schwoob. Jake bought this business which was previously known as Forbes Trading Company. In 1913, that original wood-framed structure was destroyed in a catastrophic fire. Rather than close the business, Schwoob chose to rent the Iowa Store until construction could be completed on his new building. Cody Trading would remain in business until 1961.

Cody Trading Company was the big box store of its time with the slogan "We Sell Everything."

Interior Pictures
Cody Trading Company
1302-1310 Sheridan Avenue

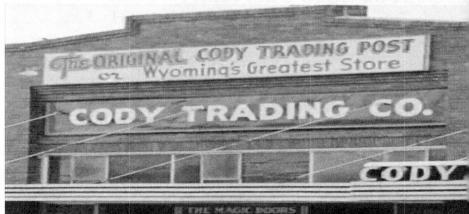

1962

1965

2018

1302-1310 Sheridan (continued)

In 1961, after Cody Trading Company closed, the building became home to Western Auto from 1962-1964.

From 1965 until around 1994 this address was Woolworth's.

Story has it Woolworth's had a pet department that sold baby alligators. Quite a few people will remember this store, the lunch counter and the ice cream sodas they served.

this storefront now houses Western Cellular, Pizza on The Run and O'Donnell Wealth Management. 68

Circa 1907

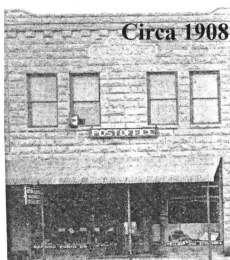
Circa 1908

1940's

1940's

1313 Sheridan Avenue

In 1906, this building was constructed for the Big Horn Lodge #36 of the Independent Order of Foresters. The original lot cost $400.

This building housed many organizations on the second floor, including the Presbyterian Church, the Masons, Eagles and, for a short time a KKK Chapter.

The original Cody Post Office was located in a tiny room in the back of the building with a small curio shop in the front of the building.

69

1950

1950's

1313 Sheridan Avenue (continued)

The front section of the building was rented out as Harding Curio. The Post Office moved out of the building in 1927 when the new Post Office building was completed on the corner of 13th and Beck Avenue.

From 1932-1964 the building was the Grocerteria, one of several grocery stores in the neighborhood. The Cody Hotel and Dining Room occupied the area where the Silver Dollar Bar patio is currently located.

1950's

1979

2009

2018

1313 Sheridan Avenue (continued)

This business became the Silver Dollar Bar in 1969 at this location after moving from 1226 Sheridan.

In 1986 a grill was added to the business and the name was changed to the Silver Dollar Bar and Grill. Around 1992 the back bar was known as Angie's bar and was owned by Pat Angelovic. In the 1990's there was a sand volleyball court where the outdoor patio is currently.

Today the Silver Dollar Bar and Grill is one of the most popular drinking establishments in Cody.

1948

1955

Circa 1966

War Surplus Store

1323 Sheridan Avenue

This building has been through multiple uses since it was constructed. In 1947-1951this storefront was home to Gamble's Hardware.

During the years of 1953-1961, this address became known as the Furniture Center. From 1964-1976 this building was the War Surplus Store, owned and operated by Jack Skates.

From 1976-1978 this address was Jack's Sports and OK Hardware

1980

1995

2002

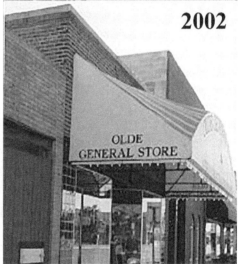

1323 Sheridan Avenue (continued)

This location became one of many locations for Sunlight Sports. They were located here for 10 years beginning in 1979.

In 1990 this storefront became home to the Olde General Store. The Olde General Store remained in business until 2001.

For a short time between 2002-2003 this was the location of Prairie Rose Art Gallery.

After this time this address was the location and storefront for North Pole West, a Christmas store until 2008.

1323 Sheridan Avenue (continued)

Between the years 2009-2011 this structure was home to Buffalo Traders.

During the years of 2011-2013 this address was the storefront for Sticks and Stones, a local boutique and furniture store.

In 2015, the building became the location for Sylvia's, a clothing store. The building now houses the storefront of Cowtown Candy, owned and operated by Kenny Lee.   74

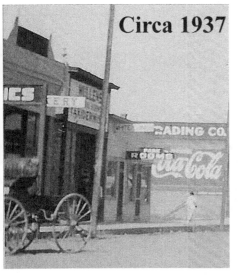
Circa 1937

Circa 1937

MULLENS
NATURAL SCIENCE
TAXIDERMISTS

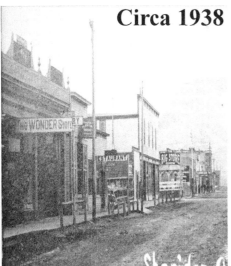
Circa 1938

1940's

Bell Plaza 1326-1348 Sheridan Avenue

This area has been home to many businesses over the years.

This address was originally home to the Amoretti Parks Company Bank.

Around 1937, this building became Mullen's Taxidermy. Prior to Mullen's, this address was home to Jess Frost's Grocery and Package Liquor Store. 1326 was home to Mountain Bell Telephone and Telegraph, before becoming Mountain Telephone Company from 1970-1982.

1908

Circa 1910

1940

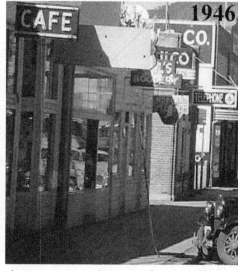

1946

1326-1348 Sheridan Avenue (continued)

The area that is now Bell Plaza has been home to several structures.

From 1900-1910, 1338 Sheridan was home to the Owl Cafe.

Between 1932-1933 this building was known as the Park Cafe. From 1947-1948 this address was home to Big Horn Radio Company.

In 1966 until 1972 these addresses housed The Fabric Shop at 1326 and Shoshone Valley Trading Company at 1348. Shoshone Valley Trading would remain in business until 1978.

1975

2018

Bell Plaza 1326-1348 Sheridan Avenue

1348 Sheridan Avenue was home to C.B. Dawson Plumbing from 1937-1941.

In 1948-1951 this was the storefront of Bill's Bootery. In 1960 it became home to Cody Saddle Company.

From 1972-1980 this address became the location for Beartooth Floral, The Fabric Shop and Shoshone Valley Trading. After the buildings were torn down, this area has become known as Bell Plaza and is now used for many community events.

Circa 1910

1960

1350 Sheridan Avenue

In 1910 this location was William Lenninger's Bakery. From 1932-1939 this building was home to Cody Bakery and then became Wigwam Bakery from 1940-1944.

In 1952-1953 this address became Neely's Sports Shop.

This building became the home of Dungan's Used Furniture Store from 1956-1963.

1983

1985

2014

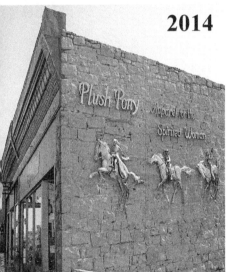

2018

1350 Sheridan Avenue (continued)

From 1974-1981 this building served as The Fabric Shop.

In the years 1982-2015 this location was the storefront of Plush Pony, a womens clothing store.

This building is currently Legend's Bookstore, Cody's only full-service bookstore.

Toggery

Circa 1935

1950's

1355 Sheridan Avenue

This building was one of the many locations that the Toggery Cleaners called home in Cody. The Toggery Cleaners originally started at 1210 Sheridan Avenue. The Toggery Cleaners would remain in business until 1994. Their slogan was "The Best Out West".

Between 1996-1997 this address was home to the Buffalo Chips Indian Art Gallery. In 1999-2000 this building became home to Shady Business.   80

1355 Sheridan Avenue (continued)

In 2001 this location became another art gallery known as Big Horn Print Gallery, which remained in business until 2010.

For a short time in 2011 this address was known as Heart Of Nature.

In 2012 this storefront became Cody Fine Art Gallery until 2013.

During 2014-2017 this structure was home to Sports HQ, a sporting goods store. In 2018 this address became Big Horn Design, a local sign and clothing design company   81

1356 Sheridan Avenue

This building was originally Safeway from 1932-1937. In 1960 this structure became Coast to Coast Hardware until 1980.

Between 1980-1986, this address was the location of Kelley's shoes, one of its many locations in Cody. During the years of 1996-2001 this building was home to Prairie Rose Art Gallery and Store.

2002

2012

2018

1356 Sheridan Avenue (continued)

During the years of 2001-2004 this building was the location for Rocky Mountain Atmosphere Art Gallery. From 2005-2006 this location was home to H & B Trading Post.

Between 2007-2009 this was the storefront of Indigo Magpie. From 2010-2017 this address was The Golden Buffalo Fine Jewelry Store, which was owned and operated by Larry Gorchesky. In 2018 this building became Yancy Interior and Home Store.

Circa 1938

Circa 1940

1976

1362 Sheridan Avenue

This building was home to F.W. Kurtz Plumbing from 1932-1940. From 1940-1953, Kurtz ran Kurtz China Store at this address. In 1978-1986, this location was the storefront of Coast To Coast Hardware. After Kelley's Shoes moved down the block the hardware store expanded taking up the whole building. Between 1986-1990, there were several other businesses at this location.

1998

1978

2018

1362 Sheridan Avenue (continued)

From 1990-1997, 1362 was The Male Room, a mens clothing store. The west end of this address became Olde Faithful Bicycles from 1992-1999.

During the years of 1997-1999 the east end of this building in the area that is now Zapata's, was home to Doug and Leslie's Clothing.

Since 2001 this address has been home to Zapata's New Mexico Style Mexican Restaurant. 85

1362 Sheridan Avenue (continued)

From 1999-2003 this location was home to Cody Custom Cycles.

In 2005 this address became Cowtown Candy Company, this business would remain here until 2015, when it was sold and moved down the street to its current location.

From 2016-2017 this structure was home to WYogurt.

In 2018 this location became Vision Stone And Tile and Budget Blinds.

1940

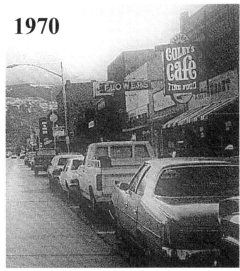
1970

1980

2018

1367 Sheridan Avenue

During the years of 1932-1953, This address was home to the Cody Enterprise. Between 1956-1966 this location was Craig's Cafe. From 1967-1989, this storefront became a popular restaurant known as Coley's Cafe.

In 1990 this building became Queen Bee Fashions, a clothing store until 1996. During the years of 1997-2005, This location was Stefan's Restaurant. Since 2006, this building has been Wyoming's Rib and Chop House.

1371 Sheridan Avenue

This location when built was the first location of J.C. Penney's in Cody. Penney's was in this location from 1932-1956.

From 1960-1961 this location would become Wyoming Automotive. After 1961 there were many businesses at this address including a travel agency, real estate offices and Western Auto.

1371 Sheridan Avenue (continued)

In 2016, this location became the Orchid Boutique which would remain in business for a short time.

From 2017-2018 this address became home to Cody Custom Designs, a local t shirt company. This business would remain through the summer.

Since March of 2018 this location has been home to Daisy Farm Decor and Cody Lodging Company upstairs.

Circa 1961

1978

1981

1385-1391 Sheridan Avenue

From 1932- 1933 this location was the office of Buffalo Bill Oil Company. In 1940 this address became the Chief Service Station and would remain in business under several different owners until 1977.

During the years 1978-1979 this structure became Chief Mobil Service Station. After 1979, the building was remodeled and became Temptations Restaurant on the west end and the Stake Out Restaurant on the east end.

2006

2018

1385-1391 Sheridan Avenue (continued)

In 1984 this address became known as La Comida Mexican Restaurant. From 2016-2017 this restaurant was remodeled and became home to the Bucking Burger Restaurant.

Since May 1, 2017 this building has been home to Gasthaus Cardi, owned and operated by Chuck and Ricki Struemke.

1950's

1950's

2018

1401 Sheridan Avenue

In 1937, Bud Webster opened Webster Chevrolet at this location. After several years, he was able to purchase the Ford Dealership next door. Bud would expand Webster's to include the whole corner. Webster also owned the Coca Cola Bottling Plant behind this location until 1962. Webster's remained here until 1951. In 1992, Shoshone First National Bank built their new building at this location. The bank was bought by Wells Fargo in 2008.

1940 · Circa 1976

1980

2018

1402 Sheridan Avenue

From 1936-1941, this address was the location of Western Paint and Electric. Between the years of 1947-1977, this building was home to Dungan's Furniture Store.

In 1978, this storefront became Cody Furniture Company. The furniture company would remain in business until 1986.

Beginning in 1993, this building became Love's Gifts and Other Things. Love's moved from this building in 2006. Since 2007, this storefront has been Mountain Home Interiors.

1983

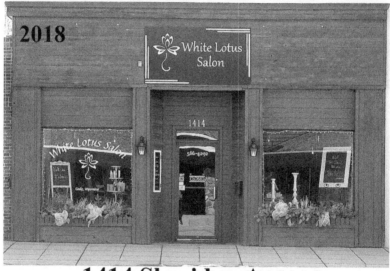

2018

White Lotus Salon

1414 Sheridan Avenue

From 1932-1953, this address was home to Mountain States Power. Between 1981-1985, this storefront was home to Wagon Wheel Gallery and Art Supplies.

In 1994, this became Big Horn Gallery, before becoming Country Flowers in 2002.

From 2012-2014, this storefront was the location of Rejuvalese Salon and Day Spa. Since 2016, this address has been White Lotus Salon.

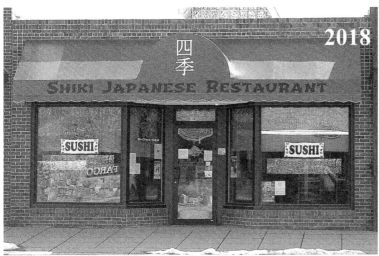

1420 Sheridan Avenue

In 1948-1972 This storefront was the location of Valley Motor Supply.

From 1974-1993, this was the location of Yellowstone Electric. Between 2002-2003, this store was known as Construction Concepts. For a short time in 2006, this storefront was Rocky Mountain Vivarium.

Since 2006, this storefront has been home to Shiki Japanese Restaurant.

1426 Sheridan Avenue

In 1994 this building was home to Mountain People.

From 1995-1996, this location was Water Rush, a garden fountain shop.

In 2014 this address became First National Bank and Trust.

In 2014 the name of the bank was changed to First Bank of Wyoming. Since 2018, this building has been First Bank a division of Glacier Bank of Montana.

1938

1950

1962

2018

1438 Sheridan Avenue

The Ross Hotel was built on this location prior to 1930. The Ross Hotel would remain at this location until the mid 1960's.

This address housed many businesses over the years including Ken's Flowers, Northfork Anglers and several clothing stores. This location is now home to an office complex with Charles Winninger, Thompson Law Firm, Level Four Wealth Management and several other businesses.

This building is now known as the Frontier Building.

1950

1963

2009

1450 Sheridan Avenue

This string of businesses originally started out as one long building encompassing all the addresses.

During the years of 1948-1966, this building was home to Shoshone Garage, which over the years would sell Dodge, Chrysler, Plymouth and Desoto automobiles.

From 1972-1986, this building would become home to Pacific Power, the local power company. In 2002 Domino's Pizza opened in the east end of the string of three businesses. In 2009 the east end location became home to Mr. Bob's Game Room and Dragon's Lair Games.

2009

2015

2018

1450 Sheridan Avenue (continued)

During the years of 2009-2014, this address was the storefront for Needlework Paradise, a sewing shop.

In the summer of 2015 this building was home to Cody Cupcake Company, a local bakery owned and operated by Sara Struemke. Since 2016 this has been home to The Beta Coffeehouse.

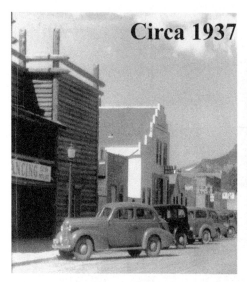

Circa 1937

1452 Sheridan Avenue

Wolfville Hall was a large prominent all wood dance hall and community entertainment facility built at this location in the early 1920's. It was built to resemble an old fort that would have been seen in many towns in the western United States.

Community dances were held in this building on Wednesday and Saturday nights. This building was also used for many private events that were held in Cody at the time, including weddings, parties, anniversaries and class reunions.

1940

1940

2018

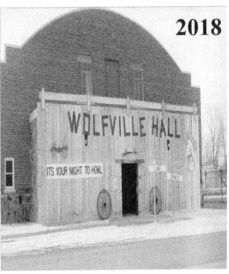
2018

1452 Sheridan Avenue (continued)

Wolfville Hall would remain in this location until July 15, 1940, when the building was destroyed in a catastrophic fire.

A new building would be built on this property and would serve as several coffeee shops, restaurants, a donut shop, a cupcake bakery and even a video arcade. The area is now home to The Beta Coffee House and Thai Thai restaurant. Both businesses have been in this location since 2016. Wolfville Hall is now recreated each year in February in the Cody Auditorium, for the Buffalo Bill Birthday Ball. 101

1955

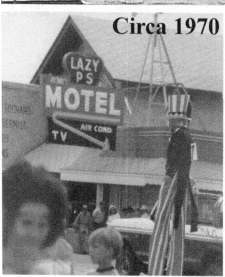

Circa 1970

2009

1452 Sheridan Avenue (continued)

This location was originally built as the Lazy PS Motel and the Lazy PS Court. Both of these Businesses were owned and operated by Pete Shultz from 1952-1970.

Later, these buildings would be torn down and a new set of buildings would be built on the property.

From 1987-2011 this storefront was home to one of Cody's popular donut shops, Daylight Donuts.

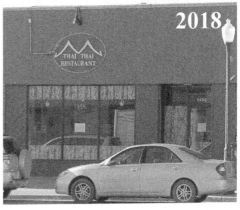

1452 Sheridan Avenue (continued)

In 2013 for a short time this storefront was a restaurant known as The Eatery.

From 2014-2016, this location was the home of Taratorrey's Grab & Go Grill. In 2016, this address became the Thai Thai Restaurant where it remains in operation today.

This building has had quite a few businesses in the building and has always been a popular location.

1940

1960's

1960's

2018

1453 &1455 Sheridan Avenue

This area was the location of Diamond Lumber from 1936-1977. In 1978 it became home to Aldrich Lumber.

From 1985 to the present this area has become Cody Motor Lodge. Between 1989-1994 the area west of the motor lodge office in front of the property, was Pizza On The Run. Since 1995 this area has housed the Smoker Friendly Cigarette Store.

 1950's

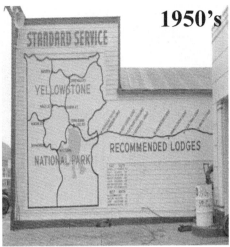 1950's

 2006

 2018

1491 Sheridan Avenue

This location was one of Cody's many gas stations that were located on Sheridan Avenue over the years. From 1932-1939 it was Red Top Standard. It went through several owners.

From 1960-1970 this address was Bud's Standard owned by Bud Fritzler. In 1987 this location became River Runners Rafting Company. This business was founded in 1967 by Buffalo Bill's great grandsons, although in a different location.

During 2007 a coffee shop known as Grizzly Creek Coffee Company was added to the building. This building is still home to both River Runners Rafting Company and Grizzly Creek Coffee Company.

Will Richard and Jess Frost

Jess and Bob Edgar
1966

1492 Sheridan (now 1456)

This business was opened early in the 1900's and was sold in 1951. This building was home to Will Richard Taxidermy. Will was a well-known taxidermist in Wyoming and also through the nation. He would even do mounts for an African safari.

Will also ran a small Cody museum, which was mostly mounts. in this building for a short time. The east side of the structure was the shop and the west side was the family home.

Circa 1968

Jess Frost 1974

Jess Frost

2009

1492 Sheridan Avenue (now 1456)

After working for and being trained by Will Richard for several years, Jess Frost purchased the shop from him. Jess would change the name to Jess Frost Taxidermy in 1952.

He would continue to run this business until 1976. He and his family lived in the west end of the structure before building a house on Newton Avenue. The west side of the shop at 1492 became the first Bargain Box location in Cody. In 1982, this property was sold and would become Wendy's.

Circa 1945

Circa 1945

2018

1503 Sheridan Avenue

This corner was a Texaco station for many years. From 1936-1945 it was Siddle Brothers Garage. This business would remain as a Texaco station until 2001. During the years of 1996-2001 this location also had an Arby's restaurant inside.

From 2010-2011 this location was Rodeo Car Wash.

Since 2011 this address has been home to Libations Liquor Store, which also includes a drive through liquor window. 108

1535 Sheridan Avenue

In 1952-1953 this building was constructed as the Westward Motel. From 1956-1976 this structure was another motel known as the Lariat Motel. During the years of 1976-2008 this was another popular bar in Cody, known as the Downtowner.

After 2008 this property as well as several connecting properties were torn down to make way for the Walgreen's Drug Store that occupies the property now.

1960

1961

1985

2010

1585 Sheridan Avenue

This corner was originally home to Park Service Station. From 1948-1953 this location was Mer Clere Motors. During the years of 1956-1977, this address was Gordon's Husky Service Station, owned and operated by Gordon Way.

From 1978-2000 this corner was home to Lynn's Husky Station. Between 2001-2008 this was the location of Bearco Texaco and Tires. Since 2010 it has been home to Walgreen's.   110

Circa 1933

Circa 1935

1937

1701 Sheridan Avenue

This area is one of the older original campground areas in Cody. The Buffalo Bill Cabin Camp was founded around 1930 or before. The area consisted of 61 cabins, several tent camping areas and several areas for camper trailers.

The Orchard Service Station operated at this location from 1936-1938. Buffalo Bill Service Station replaced it in 1938.

1701 Sheridan Avenue (continued)

The Buffalo Bill Service Station would remain in business until 1972. The Buffalo Bill Cabin Camp stayed in business until 1966, before becoming the Buffalo Bill Village from 1966-1971. The second home of the Cody Stampede rodeo grounds was to the north of Buffalo Bill Village and just behind Eastside School.

During the this era there were many other businesses in the village, including a petting zoo, several restaurants, a blacksmith shop, River Runners Raft Company, the Bandana Room, a bar and The Pioneer Playhouse, a melodrama theatre.   112

2018

2016

2018

2018

1701 Sheridan Avenue (continued)

Along the boardwalk beside the hotel office was the Sarsaparilla Saloon, which opened in 1967 and was in operation until 1972. Many melodramas and events were held in this saloon. The motel office, now the gift shop was built and opened around 1963.

Since 1974 the Holiday Inn and Comfort Inn have occupied this address. The Buffalo Bill Village and some of the original cabins are still located in the rear of the property.

1968

1968

1968

2013

17th And Sheridan Avenue

Bud Webster opened Webster Chevrolet on this corner in 1968, after having moved from 1400 Sheridan Avenue. This business would remain here until 2013, when the property was sold to Denny Menholt Chevrolet of Billings, Montana. Since 2013 it has remained as Denny Menholt Chevrolet.

**The following pages are a preview
of my next book.**

Cody Characters

William "Coach" Waller

Not much has been written concerning Bill Waller and his adventure in his life and also in Cody.

Bill was a well recognized face in Cody, but not a person that people know the history of.

Bill was born in Thompsonville, Illinois in 1911. He was involved in sports for most of the years of his life. Bill went to the University of Illinois in Champagne, Illinois.

Bill excelled at all sports, but was most adept as a football player. While at the University of Illinois he would play for Coach Bob Zupke. He continued his football career with the Los Angeles Bulldogs,New York Giants and the Brooklyn dodgers football teams. He was recognized by the Chicago Bears and the Detroit Lions. Bill played for the Lions for 2 years. He worked as a field director for a rehabilitation camp in Africa for the Red Cross. He became football coach at Cody High in 1944. In 1946 he was instrumental in founding the wrestling program at the high school level throughout Wyoming. Bill went on to coach football in Washington and at Southern Illinois University. He returned to coach again in Cody in 1953, retiring in 1957. Bill was adopted as an honorary member of both the Northern Cheyenne and Northern Arapaho Indian tribes. He was given the name he would be known by for the rest of his life "White Man Dances". He learned a lot of his Native American skills from the tribe. 117

William Waller 1938 Brooklyn Dodgers Football

1945

WILLIAM WALLER, B. A. & M. S.
Physical Education
University of Illinois

Bill "Coach" Waller

After retiring in 1957, Bill continued showcasing his Native American talents as "White Man Dances" at schools, museums and Native American events throughout the state and country. He became a physical education teacher at the middle school in Cody. When he would drive students to the recreation center, Bill would regale the students with Native American stories, artifacts that he created and would even teach then how to do wood carvings. Bill was recognized for many years in parades as "White Man Dances".

William "White Man Dances" Waller

Bill Waller was highly respected in Cody and is still remembered to this day. Stories are still being told by former friends and former students about "Coach" Waller as they knew him. Stories are often told of his elaborate wood carvings, his Native American stories, the turtle shell shields he made and the dances he taught and performed.

Bill would hold summer camps where he would teach kids the Native American ways, dances and stories as well as often performing at the Buffalo Bill Historical Center museum.

Picture Credits
All pictures listed left to right
PCA= Park County Archives

Page 7 Author, Author, Author, Author
Page 8 PCA P17-10-043, Author, Author, Author
Page 9 PCA P98-55-07, Author, Author, Author
Page 10 Author, Author, Author, Author
Page 11 Author, Author, Author, Author
Page 12 Author, PCA P87-01-04, Pca p95-46-21
Page 13 Author, Author, Author
Page 14 PCA PN86-26-08, Cutter Collection,, Author
Page15 Author, Cutter Collection, Cutter Collection, Author
Page 16 PCA P99-37-37, Frost Family Collection, Frost Family Collection
Page 17 Frost Family Collection, Author, Author, Author
Page 18 All pictures Frost Family Collection
Page 19 All pictures Frost Family Collection
Page 20 PCAP07-07-163, PCA P05-06-27, PCA P86-024-041, Author
Page 21 Author, Cutter Collection, Author
Page 22 PCA P91-27-05, PCA P05-06-19, PCA P91-27-18
Page 23 PCA P91-31-57, Author, Author, Author
Page24 Author, Author, Author, Author
Page25 Author, PCA P07-30-07, Jon Wilson, Jon Wilson
Page26 PCA P80-12-163,Author, Cutter Collection, Author
Page27 Author, Author, Frost Family Collection
Page 28 Cutter Collection, Author, Author, Author
Page 29 All pictures Frost Family Collection
Page30 Frost Family Collection, Frost Family Collection, Author
Page31 PCA P02-66-100, PCA P00-28-21, PCA P86-024-043, PCA P17-13-010
Page 32 Author, Author, Author, Author
Page 33 Author, Author, Author, Author
Page 34 Frost Family Collection, Author, PCA P01-5-441, Author
Page 35 Author, Author, Author
Page 36 PCA P86-8-18 Author, Author
Page 37 Author, Author, Cutter Collection, Author
Page 38 Author, Author, Jon Wilson, Author
Page 39 Jon Wilson, Author, Author
Page 40 Author, Author, Author, Author
Page 41 PCA P10-22-230 ,Author, PCA P9476-45, Author
Page 42 Author, Author, Author, Author
Page 43 Wilson, Wilson, Cutter Collection, Author
Page 44 Author, Author, Author,
Page 45 Cutter Collection, Author, Author, Author
Page 46 PCA P86-013-04, Author , Author, Author
Page 47 Cutter Collection, PCA P10-29-326,Author
Page 48 Author, PCA P06-10-233, Cutter Collection, Author
Page 49 PCA P05-46-14, Author, PCA P06-10-233, Cutter Collection
Page 50 Author, Author, Author, Author
Page 51 Jon Wilson, Author, Author, Author
Page 52 PCA P00-28-28, PCA P06-10-362, Author, Author
Page 53 PCA P00-06-042, PCA P15-14-19, Author, Author
Page 54 Author, Author, Jon Wilson, Author
Page 55 Cutter Collection, P06-10-360, Author, Author
Page 56 PCA P86-023-015, PCA P00-06-315, PCA P05-46-19, PCA P00-06-315
Page 57 Author, Author, Author, Author
Page 58 PCA P98-50-30, PCA P94-36-6, PCA P98-36-01, Author
Page 59 Author, PCA P94-76-32, P15-14-47 Author
Page 60 Jon Wilson, Linda Boggiano, Linda Boggiano, Author

Picture Credits
All Pictures Listed left to right
PCA= Park County Archives

Page 61 PCA P95-18-156, Author, Author, Author
Page 62 Cutter Collection, Cutter Collection, Author, Author
Page 63 PCA P99-42-06, Author, PCA P97-67-22, Author
Page 64 Author, Author, Author,
Page 65 PCA P02-66-69, PCA P05-06-16, Author, PCA P01-54-59
Page 66 PCA P97-7-101, PCA P 97-7-02, PCA P97-7-05, PCA P01-5-457, PCA P01-5-468, PCA P11-7-2,PCA P 11-7-1
Page 67 PCA P11-7-6, PCA P11-7-7, PCA P11-7-12, PCA P11-7-9, PCA P11-7-10, PCA P11-7-14, PCA P11-7-16, PCA P11-7-19, PCA P11-7-20
Page 68 Author, Author, PCA P17-13-02, Author
Page 69 Author, Author, Author, Author
Page 70 PCA P97-67-22, Author, PCA P94-76-37
Page 71 Author, Author, Author, Author
Page72 Author, Author, Author
Page 73 PCA P02-93-095, Author, PCA P)6-10-375
Page 74 Author, Author, Author
Page 75 Author, PCA P98-015-06, PCA P02-66-05, Author
Page 76 Jon Wilson, PCA P02-66-05, Author, Author
Page 77 Author, Author
Page 78 Cutter Collection, Author,
Page 79 Author, Author, Author, Author
Page 80 Author, Author
Page 81 Author, Author, Author
Page 82 Cutter Collection, Cutter Collection, Author
Page 83 Author, Author, Author
Page 84 PCA P10-29-165, Author, Author, Jon Wilson
Page 85 Author, Cutter Collection, Author
Page 86 Author, Author
Page 87 Author, Author, Author, Author
Page 88 Author, Author, Author
Page 89 Author Author, Author, Author
Page 90 Author, Author, Author
Page 91Author, Author, Cutter Collection
Page 92 PCA P17-13-004 Author, Author, Author
Page 93 P01-47-2,   ,Cutter Collection, Author
Page 94 Cutter Collection, Author
Page 95 Author, Author
Page 96 P06-10-367, Author, Author
Page 97 Author , Cutter Collection, Cutter Collection, Author
Page 98 Author, Cutter Collection, Author
Page 99 Author, Sara Struemke, Author
Page 100Author, PCA P86-34-050, PCA P15-14-70,
Page 101 PCA P94-76-41 PCA P94-36-14, Author, Author
Page 102 Author, Author, Author
Page 103 Author, Author, Author, Author
Page 104 PCA P86-4-03, Author, PCA P98-55-11, Author
Page 105 Author, Author, Author, Author
Page 106 All Images Frost Family Collection
Page 107 Frost Family Collection, Frost Family Collection, Frost Family Collection, Author
Page 108 Author, Author, Author, Author
Page 109 Author, Author, Author
Page 110 Author, PCA P04-37-024, Author, Author
Page 111 Author, Author, Author
Page 112 PCA P01-5-412, PCA P01-5-412
Page 113 Author, Author, Author, Sheldon Family Collection, Author
Page 114 Author, Author, Author, Author

Picture Credits
All Pictures Listed left to right
PCA= Park county Archives

Page 115 Author, Author,Author, Author
Page 117 Sheldon Family Collection
Page 118 Author, Sheldon Family Collection, PCA P09-42-462
Page 119 Sheldon Family Collection, Author, Sheldon Family Collection, Sheldon Family Collection

Made in the USA
Las Vegas, NV
12 July 2023

74564425R00073